"Be who you are
And say what you feel
Because those who mind
Don't matter
And those who matter
Don't mind."

DR SEUSS

Exploring self identity

Directed by
Marksteen Adamson

Jack Adamson
Photography – Marksteen Adamson

Contents

Introduction

"Conditions of worth are the expectations we think
we must meet in order for other people to accept us
as worthy of their love or positive regard."

Carl Rogers (1902-1987)

We naturally take on board other people's values
and ideas of how we should be. If we don't examine
why we think the things we think, then we soon
lose clarity of who we really are. To find our true
worth and identity, we need to first separate out
what we believe to be right for ourselves and then
resist the expectations of people around us.

PEEL is an exploration of self-identity and is the
culmination of a three-year study working with
groups of young people, using photography and
poetry, to explore their identity and uncover who
they are rather than just what they look like.

TRYING TO ESTABLISH A TRUE IDENTITY... HAS NEVER BEEN HARDER FOR YOUNG PEOPLE.

Social media, self-expression and self-identity
present a growing problem for young people.
Trying to establish a true identity, whilst finding
themselves within a 'selfie' culture of carefully
curated Facebook and Instagram lives, has never
been harder.

**PEEL TEACHES
US TO TAKE THE
TIME TO LISTEN
TO EACH OTHER.**

The overall objective of the PEEL project is to inspire young people to connect on a deeper level by asking each other a series of searching questions, face to face. They listen to the responses, and work towards a distilled summary that culminates in a poem that describes and encapsulates something about the person they have spent time with. Participants can then start thinking, together, about what the photographic portrait could be, referencing an experience or emotion that represents an aspect or point of view of the individual.

**PEEL IS THE
BEGINNING OF
A DISCOVERY
PROCESS THAT
GOES BACK TO
A TIME WHEN
WE SPENT MORE
'REAL' TIME
TOGETHER.**

By taking a break from endless 'short bursts' of online communications and instead engaging with each other face to face, PEEL teaches us to take the time to listen to one other. Using a series of PEEL questions – and also adding their own – the students uncover and discover new stories and interesting narratives about each other that have shaped their lives. They discover each others' hopes, strengths and fears to gain an authentic glimpse into their developing identities and a better understanding of who they are.

PEEL is not the only answer. But it is the beginning of a discovery process that goes back to a time when we spent more 'real' time together, before we became addicted to our smart-phones.

Back then, we were looking up at the stars and into each other's eyes, making connections, discovering and sharing wonders. We learned how to deal with awkward silent moments and abandon our shyness by talking to each other at bus stops and in silent lifts. We spent time getting to know each other, time that taught us to be patient and gave us wisdom, dignity and the meaning of real community. Above all it gave us hope. We learned to be still, how to be alone and the art of sometimes switching off and doing literally nothing.

Then the world changed. Streets and bars were full of lit-up faces constantly looking down into the palm of their hands, silently bumping into things and each other on their way to a WiFi friendly zone. Couples out together for dinner were in separate online worlds, parents at home were glued to social media, whilst toddlers entertained and nourished their curiosity on tablet screens. The parks where kids once played were now empty, the bus stops and lifts stayed silent. We no longer wanted to connect or step beyond our shyness.

STREETS AND BARS WERE FULL OF LIT-UP FACES CONSTANTLY LOOKING DOWN INTO THE PALM OF THEIR HANDS.

We can't stop young people using social media and playing online, but we can help them moderate by guiding them towards a greater understanding of who they are and what they could become. Once they have a deeper and more positive individual expression of their own unique identity, then we can inspire them to put down their devices more frequently and enjoy life with each other in the physical world. This in turn inspires a richer understanding and compassion towards each other and builds resilience in young people to help them make better decisions and navigate through an ever-growing virtual reality.

INSTEAD OF TELLING THEM HOW TO BEHAVE, TAKE THEM ON A JOURNEY THAT CHANGES THEIR BEHAVIOURS.

There will never be an electronic or online application for empathy. There is only the human version and the application of that must happen face to face. There is no substitute for a 'person to person' interaction if we want to build meaningful and authentic relationships in our lives.

Rather than tell us how to behave, PEEL takes us on a journey that hopes to change our behaviour towards a more positive world of genuine interaction.

Marksteen Adamson

STUDIES

1. George Pack
Poetry – Tiana Mvula-Dodd
Photography – Tiana Mvula-Dodd

Turn off the TV at 5:30
because it takes his glee.
He never enjoyed watching the news,
it shows all the bad views.
Change the difference in wealth,
money is less important than health.
George likes to be
in places where he can be free.
When asked his best memory,
it was Mount Snowdon with family.

2. Thaïs Donovan
Poetry – Tom Rigby
Photography – Tom Rigby

When she learnt
she was moving to England,
feelings of anger and fear arose.

On the plane,
uneasy and consumed by dread
her eyes transfixed on the ocean below.

Finding her feet,
she learnt the vowels
and consonants and verbs of
the English language from scratch.

But now,
surrounded by her reconstruction
she is satisfied with

  Mon chez

    moi hors

      de chez moi.

3. Henry Denyer
Poetry – Prudence Bond
Photography – Prudence Bond

As he wakes
the morning breaks,
he's never too late
to the world he makes.
His mind's been blown
by the things he's seen,
stepping through places
only others could dream.

When dancing in the love
of his friends around,
he's apologetic
to a new-found frown.
With music running
in his rubber soles,
the world lifts up
his mortal soul,
lets colour fill
his wondering eyes,
leave every day
to bring a new surprise.

The man above loves the world he owns:
the time is now, this bird has flown.

4. Timothy Niblett
Poetry – Sarah Caitlin Leckebusch
Photography – Sarah Caitlin Leckebusch

Given the opportunity to change
I wouldn't
I am happy in who I am, I am free being me.

Given the chance to travel
I'd fly away
move far, start a family, live the dream.

Given the time to recover
take my fear
the loneliness, the throbbing pain of broken bones.

Given the choice of company
I'll take it
inspire me, make me ponder and think.

I've got the chance to live
I'll seize it
I'll do what it takes

I'll work
and I'll enjoy
the process
of being alive.

5. Tiana Mvula-Dodd
Poetry – George Pack
Photography – George Pack

Gleichberechtigung.

Igualdad.

Égalité.

Equality.

This is what I want.

This is what we need.

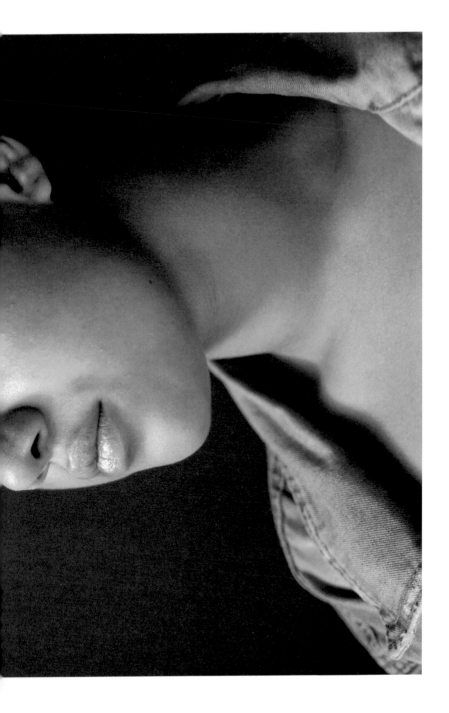

6. Felix McCartney
Poetry – Zion Davidson
Photography – Zion Davidson

Loneliness would be
inevitable if you were the last person on Earth,
but what if you could change that?

If you were completely alone in the world,
the term 'making friends' would have a very
different meaning.

You wouldn't be getting to know the person,
you would be making them in order to know them.

Robotic friends,
something many of us
dream of in the future.

Humanity is irreplaceable.

7. Claudia Naylor
Poetry – Will Bliss Carter
Photography – Holly Isherwood

a free spirit once wandered the earth
learning wisdom from the people
and feeling free on home turf

her nature an ever-growing Shangri-La
running forever wild and bizarre

ear of the unknown
in time will be shown
the future is for wishing
but now the clock is ticking

no regrets for the things unseen
time is on your side
and it's all in your dreams

rebel to the life
if this is your goal
don't ever think
you're too old

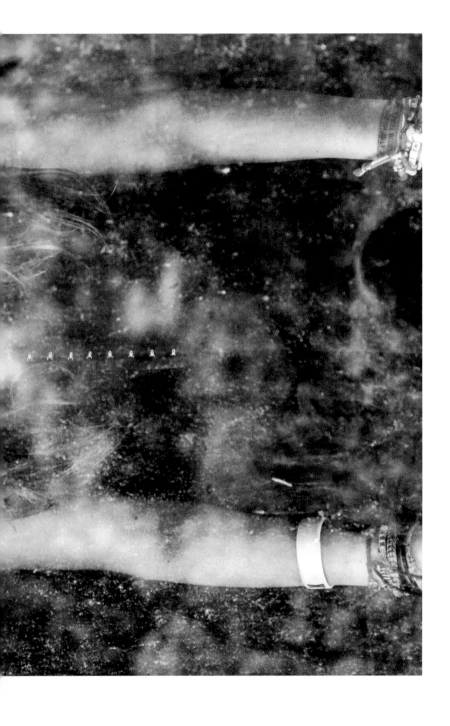

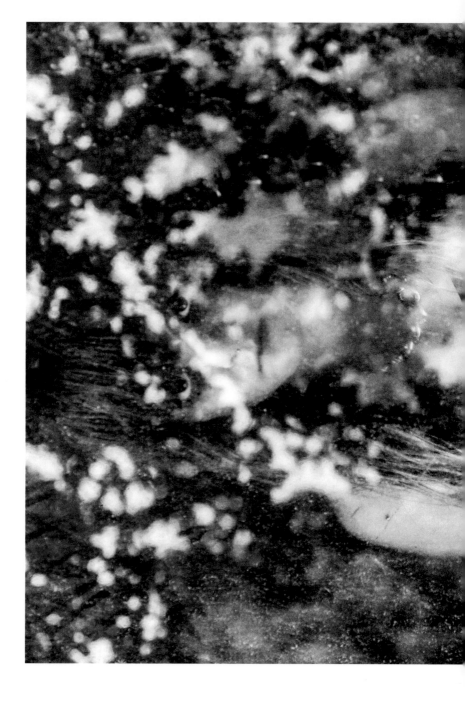

8. George Adamson
Poetry – Bryony Collishaw
Photography – Bryony Collishaw

plastic people
fake personas
swallow reality

    the joys of creativity
    the shine of laughter
    the spontaneity of invention

I can
  create happiness
   a few funny doodles
    some superheroes
     and the colour blue

I add
  photography
   a few bad jokes
    and a trip to Wales

9. Marcelina Podolska
Poetry – Oliver Thompson
Photography – Oliver Thompson

My life,
a pocket-sized
stint of time.
A toothpick in the
jaws of reality.

But I've had aspirations,
ever since I was young.
I've had numerous
views about the
state of the future.

Journalism was my dream
but time was taken up
by the reality of anxiety.
As it turned, songs echoed
in the back of my head.

Solitude never ceased
but tides shifted and
the anthem was snuffed out
of its flickering being.
Time ticked on
and the future
always promised.

10. Charles Tucker
Poetry – Natalie Thomas
Photography – Tomas André

He can't really remember
the earliest –
but there were open fields in Somerset
and a tractor he used to drive sometimes.

Well – America, maybe.
He shows me a picture of a 1962 Corvette.

The worst? Probably
when he fell off his bike and distorted his spine.
Yeah, he remembers –
tarmac on bare skin, stones tight in a wound
like the smell of diesel
behind the eyes.

Hazy. A memory. Three years back.
Systems delaying.

The quiet.

But it's ok now. He tells me

red is his favourite, the kind of red
they paint cars with and no,
he gets on with them well
but it's healthy to argue, to talk.

11. Zion Davidson
Poetry – Felix McCartney
Photography – Felix McCartney

Listening, reading, looking
through my PC screen.
Questions, fact and fiction.
What do these likes mean?
I looked it up on Google,
found out what it meant.
I wanted to know where he was,
where he went.
I found out his location,
what he likes to do.

The internet shows us everyone.
Privacy is dead.

12. Bryony Collishaw
Poetry – George Adamson
Photography – George Adamson

The world's outlook
on the things you do
and the way you do them:

music and retiring
into yourself.

The peace seen through
a green, wide angled view.

A moving image
and childish colours.

Three hours spent in the dark
looking back on that summer.

13. James Miller
Poetry – George Kitching
Photography – Catherine Miller

He listened to the ocean,
she told him where to go.
The tide swept him in.

He sought to explore,
        to collect,
        and to create something timeless.

So he went
onto the next opportunity,
the next adventure.

14. Sam Shute
Poetry – Gulalai Maroofkhel
Photography – Gulalai Maroofkhel

This isn't a land of milk and honey.
It's a mosh pit filled with screams
so defiant they could break a thousand mirrors.
But I'm at complete ease here,
you could blame it on the liquor.
My dizzy, dizzy mind sinks
into the drums that pound deafeningly,
replacing my heartbeat,
igniting vibrations like the start of a hurricane.
There isn't a second of silence to grasp,
as the sweet sound of lyrics leave lips
in a mass of bodies.
I'm oblivious to the abundance of sweat
coating their skin
or the fatigue that consumes them.
I come down from my high
and the lights dim low,
a quiet ringing in my ears.
This is home to me.

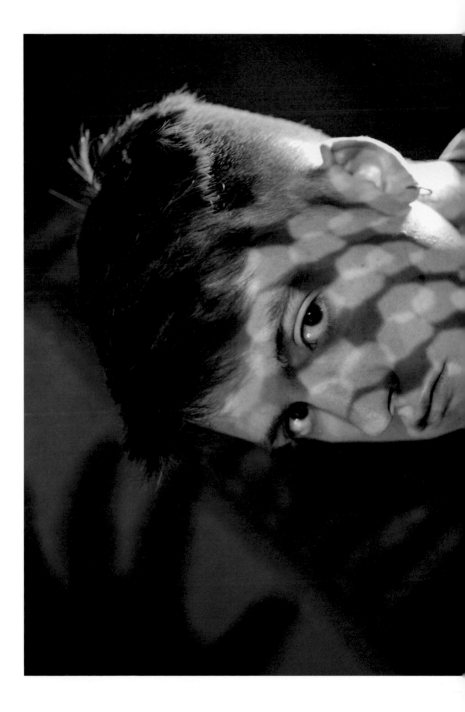

15. Lucy Thompson
Poetry – George Ovenden
Photography – George Ovenden

alone I stand
as I watch light
fight a losing battle

night's charcoal
fangs sink into
the sun's flesh

a web of black
is spun
across the sky
being thrown down
by the smoking beasts
their ominous
brick bodies
blocking my last
glimpse of hope

the warm
calming flames
lick my fingers
for the last time
as I become
engulfed

16. Oliver Hollick-Hemus
Poetry – Erin Saunders
Photography – Erin Saunders

Wind screamed in my eyes.
Roof to roof without a fear,
I took a break
from reality.
Every cell in my body
defying gravity.
Fear crept through
like a figure in the night.
With all my strength
I held back the fright.
The roof tiles slipped,
crushed with each tread.
My heart kick started.
With the feelings of dread
I...

J
    U

        M

          P

           E

            D

             !

17. Jessica Davies
Poetry – James Miller
Photography – James Miller

I create your dreams
they perceive as screens

all the world's a scene
living on reflections
skipping on the surface
of the places I've been

and I only wish I knew
a rose-tinted view

18. Florence Jewell
Poetry – Will Hancock
Photography – Will Hancock

So I asked some questions to F. Jewell
to find out what she thinks is cool.
Dreaming about books, art, treasure and loot,
an on ongoing journey,
this is her pursuit.

What inspires her and what makes her smile?
She answered 'going abroad and travelling miles.'

Seeing each culture and flying the flight,
stargazing at the blue light of the night.

It was a camping trip in the wild,
the girl was only a child,
exploring the world and enjoying the ride
while she looked up at the trees swaying
side to side.

19. Caleb Etheredge
Poetry – Sindi Rudevica
Photography – Sindi Rudevica

Strokes of acrylic,
the flow of the paintbrush.
Fears forgotten,
a lion appears on the paper,
the kaleidoscope of its mane,
vibrant maroon, golden, yellow.
Concentrating on the emerald eyes,
reflecting his own.
The movement of paint,
a performance of the mind.
Each paw emerges from the brush's tip,
strong and determined.
They walk across the paper's skin.
The mind escaping.

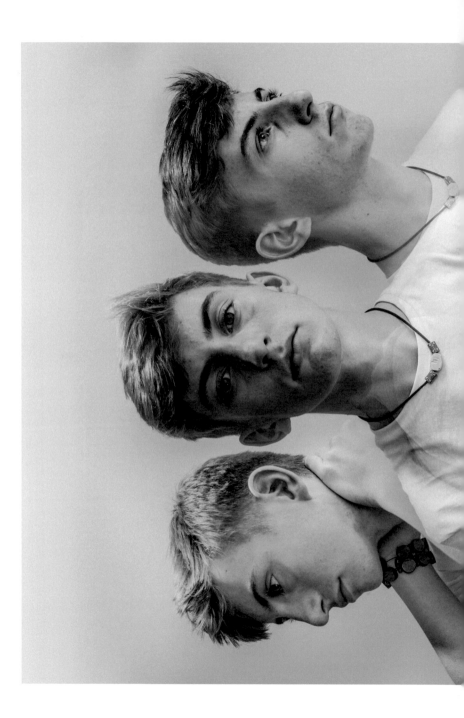

20. Oliver Thompson
Poetry – Marcelina Podolska
Photography – Marcelina Podolska

132 miles before
>*the bitter-sweet sound of the radio*
>*led me into a blissful void,*
>*its sweet sounds*
>*putting me*
>*at instant ease.*

132 miles later
>*I'm sat in sinful silence*
>*my solitude is accompanied*
>*by boxes of nostalgia*
>*my mistaken innocence*
>*my hiraeth*
>*the sound of my uncle's acoustic guitar.*

It echoes in my head
as I grieve on those authentic streets
where empty blue skies are replaced
with clouds of cigarette smoke.

Hiraeth: a bitter-sweet word itself,
which can be found
at the comfort
and switch
of a radio.

21. Erin Saunders
Poetry – Oliver Hollick-Hemus
Photography – Oliver Hollick-Hemus

Sometimes, warriors hit the ground
with a face full of snow.
I pick myself up.

Music in my ears
teaching me to be brave.
She sings 'I am a survivor.'
I'll keep my head up
and start again.

My new start and future life
will be with kids and a husband.
But I will always know
I am a warrior.

22. Prudence Bond
Poetry – Indy Roberts
Photography – Marksteen Adamson

I wasn't pushed into living
climbed over my twin sister
couldn't read the order of appearance
behold - your first daughter!

Light – and lots of open faces
I didn't care at all for waiting
an absent prompting
a lullaby? – nothing!

I screamed – loud enough for him to hear
but he had left before the news

was it wrong of me
to never care for rules?
When rules are walls
that block an ocean's view?

I go to stand before the sea
throw up – throw out fists full of words
the waves return with arms of sand
and stones that others came to throw.

I learned to live without sandwiches made by mum,
girls and sticky-rainbow-chewing-gum.

23. George Kitching
Poetry – George Ovenden
Photography – George Ovenden

Up here,

>*the anarchy looks peaceful;*
>*no noise can reach me.*
>
>*The wind shakes my hair,*
>
>*and away from the chaos I soar.*

24. Sindi Rudevica
Poetry – Caleb Etheredge
Photography – Caleb Etheredge

Her favourite colour is white,
the sea-foam surrounding the shells,
the clouds lining the hills.

Her favourite colour is black,
her coffee, just before school.
Black tops and trousers,
they go with anything.

Her favourite colour is yellow,
the sandy shore back when she couldn't swim,
yellow like the flowers arranged in her hair.

But what if there was no colour?
No people,
no anything?
I think she'd scream

but I can't be sure.

25. Gulalai Maroofkhel
Poetry – Sam Shute
Photography – Sam Shute

Life at home is too monotonous,
too simple, too dull, too plain.
She's dependent on the busyness,
further opportunities down every lane.
She's trapped inside the suburbs
with concrete jungle dreams
a breath of fresh industrial air
concealed in city scenes.

26. Catherine Miller
Poetry – Tom Sadler
Photography – Tom Sadler

the waves crash as in their nature
and I drift watching from under
blue hills forming and exploding
a battle repeating with little conclusion

the waves submerge
my whole body
their blue cloaking the sun
and the open sky and air

moving up
the waves yield to my arms
the current lulls under my splash
and the harmony of the waves dies
as I wipe the salt from my eyes

27. George Ovenden
Poetry – Lucy Thompson
Photography – Lucy Thompson

1:   *Faces stare out at me from a poster.*
      They are reflective, vacant, black.

0:   *Darkness floods the room.*
      It is thick and still and quiet.

1:   *Darkness brings a dim snarl of*
      white noise. Its voices rise and fall
      in a language I don't understand.

0:   *Static seeps away and we are dark again.*

1:   *Through the crack in my wardrobe*
      they stand with backs turned away.
      They have stopped talking.

0:   *Darkness again. We are alone.*
      It is thick and still and quiet.

28. Louissa Leal
Poetry – Natalie Thomas
Photography – Tomas André

night. the garden. blackbirds in the plum tree
chant, throw shadows against the walls.
in her house, she works out the sounds.
the washing machine sighs in circles. the floor,
wheezes and so close
the strip of light under the door, flickering.
something moves across the landing.
Q. what are you most afraid of?
A. being alone in the house
when it's dark. she contemplates open curtains
on morning light.

29. Sarah Caitlin Leckebusch
Poetry – Mirren Derby
Photography – Timothy Niblett

*Change none
of the things
that people
overlook.*

*Searching through charity shops
finding unexpected treasures,
sisters change.*

*We interlocked,
arms and hair.
And through
tangled bath times
and hugs and
bluey green moments
we are still linked.*

30. Jack Adamson
Poetry – Sophie Croft
Photography – Sophie Croft

Beneath the ice-skin of the reservoir,
he aches for the pain to leave.
Gasping for air
he tries to overthrow
the cold water
and his fear.

In the surrounding woodland
life breathes heavily,
and the trees desperately
try to prize him,
pulling, twisting, grasping.

In the serene breeze
he glides out of the water,
revived by the tranquil forest.

List of images

1. George Pack
Poetry & Photography –
Tiana Mvula-Dodd

2. Thaïs Donovan
Poetry & Photography – Tom Rigby

3. Henry Denyer
Poetry & Photography – Prudence Bond

4. Timothy Niblett
Poetry & Photography –
Sarah Caitlin Leckebusch

5. Tiana Mvula-Dodd
Poetry & Photography – George Pack

6. Felix McCartney
Poetry & Photography – Zion Davidson

7. Claudia Naylor
Poetry – Will Bliss Carter
Photography – Holly Isherwood

8. George Adamson
Poetry & Photography – Bryony Collishaw

9. Marcelina Podolska
Poetry & Photography – Oliver Thompson

10. Charles Tucker
Poetry – Natalie Thomas
Photography – Tomas André

11. Zion Davidson
Poetry & Photography – Felix McCartney

12. Bryony Collishaw
Poetry & Photography – George Adamson

13. James Miller
Poetry – George Kitching
Photography – Catherine Miller

14. Sam Shute
Poetry & Photography – Gulalai Maroofkhel

15. Lucy Thompson
Poetry & Photography – George Ovenden

16. Oliver Hollick-Hemus
Poetry & Photography – Erin Saunders

17. Jessica Davies
Poetry & Photography – James Miller

18. Florence Jewell
Poetry & Photography – Will Hancock

19. Caleb Etheredge
Poetry & Photography – Sindi Rudevica

20. Oliver Thompson
Poetry & Photography –
Marcelina Podolska

21. Erin Saunders
Poetry & Photography –
Oliver Hollick-Hemus

22. Prudence Bond
Poetry – Indy Roberts
Photography – Marksteen Adamson

23. George Kitching
Poetry & Photography – George Ovenden

24. Sindi Rudevica
Poetry & Photography – Caleb Etheredge

25. Gulalai Maroofkhel
Poetry & Photography – Sam Shute

26. Catherine Miller
Poetry & Photography – Tom Sadler

27. George Ovenden
Poetry & Photography – Lucy Thompson

28. Louissa Leal
Poetry – Natalie Thomas
Photography – Tomas André

29. Sarah Caitlin Leckebusch
Poetry – Mirren Derby
Photography – Timothy Niblett

30. Jack Adamson
Poetry & Photography – Sophie Croft

REFLECTIONS

"It's really easy to make
judgements about
people and exaggerate
them."

James Miller

"From the process of
interviewing another
person I learned the
importance of listening."

Lucy Thompson

"I realised how easy it is to work
as a team, and how a simple piece
of poetry can show who someone
is easily."

Andrew Findlay

"I've learnt that I can take good
photos if I have to and that I can use
information from someone to create
a poem. Furthermore, that I can work
well with different people."

Sindi Rudevica

"I learnt that I can write a poem, which I'm very
happy about because when I first started I didn't
think I would be able to."

Molly Knight

"I have been inspired by the photography
and might reconsider it for part of my
Art GCSE course. In addition to this,
I will also consider Art for A - level."

Oliver Berry

"I learnt about lighting, different
angles and how much of a difference
this makes."

Tiana Mvula-Dodd

"I learnt a lot about Felix during the PEEL project,
such as his fear of open waters, his passion for
graphic projects and maths which sadly, I cannot
relate to."

Zion Davidson

"I learnt about the impact of social
media, my self-perception and how
I should alter and change it using the
skills taught within these workshops."

Thaïs Donovan

"Writing the poem was actually quite simple to understand because of the questions we asked. I found it quite easy to find a theme for the poem. Also, we had a lot of help for both the poetry and photography sections."

Florence Jewell

"Seeing all the ideas on the pin boards at the end of the week, I was really surprised at what could be achieved when I put my mind on something. Also being in an environment that encouraged people to push limits and step outside of their comfort zones."

Lucy Thompson

"From Becca talking about me in her poem it made me realise that my life isn't as normal as I thought it was."

Sam Gibson

"I have learnt that if I try doing more, I will become more confident."

Oliver Berry

"What I found interesting was the interview process, writing poetry for the first time, relaxed atmosphere, working with a variety of people."

James Miller

"I learnt that with some help I can actually write a half decent poem."

Becca Chesworth

"Lucy likes the sunset and the colour orange, dislikes the unknown and wished she had tried harder in year 10 for her GCSEs."

George Ovenden

"I feel like I got to know Tom quite well because he told me about his past and his greatest fears and other things which you wouldn't usually ask someone when it's the first time you've met them. However, I know that I didn't really know him that well because I only met him for a few days... so it was really bizarre to write a poem based on him and his emotions."

Catherine Miller

"I am a lot more capable of writing poems that I thought I would be and this experience has helped me cement my passion for photography."

Sam Shute

VITAL STATISTICS

1

PHYSICAL HEADSPACE

How much do our young people engage with the physical
environment around them? How much time is spent in 'real'
interaction with friends, family and the natural environment
and how is this behaviour changing over time?

2

DIGITAL HEADSPACE

Technology is ubiquitous in our society; we are all exposed to
ever-increasing levels of sophistication and output from our devices.
The more we use technology the more demanding it seems to become.
How is this upsurge in usage affecting our young people?

3

EMOTIONAL HEADSPACE

What are the issues closest to the hearts of young people today?
How are the internet and social media affecting them emotionally
and what do their online activities reveal about their sense of
identity and self-expression?

PHYSICAL HEADSPACE

Going outside

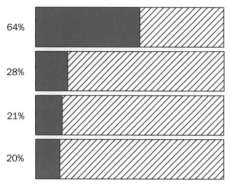

64%

28%

21%

20%

64% of children today play outside less than once a week,

28% haven't been on a country walk in the last year,

21% have never been to a farm and...

...20% have never once climbed a tree.

Survey, Eden TV, 2010

43%

The distance our children stray from home on their own has shrunk by 90% since the 70s; 43% of adults think a child shouldn't play outdoors unsupervised until the age of 14.

Survey, Eden TV, 2010

21% of children today regularly play outside, compared with 71% of their parents' generation.

More children are now admitted to British hospitals for injuries falling out of bed than falling out of trees.

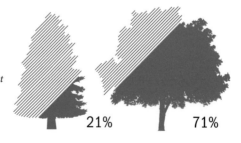

21%

71%

Survey, Eden TV, 2010

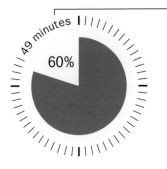

The average UK family spends 49 minutes a day together.

One in 10 spend no more than two hours a week together.

More than **60%** of parents said that when they are together, time is normally spent in silence in front of the TV, at the cinema, playing computer games or glued to a mobile or tablet.

Poll, National Family Week, 2010

1/5

A fifth of parents regularly struggle to get their children out of their bedrooms or away from gadgets like consoles and phones...

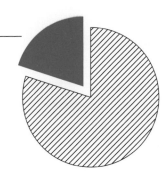

3/4

...while more than three quarters of those studied were familiar with the problem.

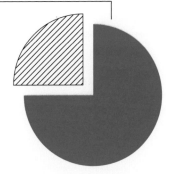

Research, Highland Spring, 2015

⅓

A third of British children aged 12 to 15 admitted they do not have a good balance between screen time and other activities.

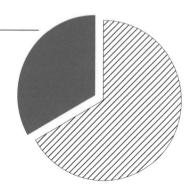

Survey, Eden TV, 2010

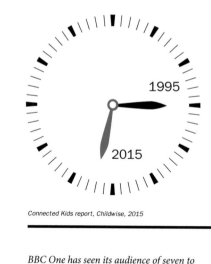

Children aged five to 16 spend an average of six and a half hours a day in front of a screen compared with around three hours in 1995.

Connected Kids report, Childwise, 2015

BBC One has seen its audience of seven to 16-year-olds drop from over 80% in 1995 to just over 40% in 2014. ITV's audience follows a similar trajectory.

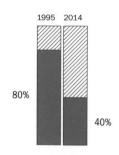

Connected Kids report, Childwise, 2015

A recent survey of 1,500 parents found that, on average, UK children own their first mobile phone by the age of seven, followed by a tablet aged eight and a smart-phone aged 10.

7Y   8Y   10Y

Survey, Opinium, 2016

The average millennial is expected to take 25,700 selfies in his or her lifetime.

25,700

Report: Now Sourcing and Frames Direct, 2015

Insecurity among young people - UK
Topic waves from 2010 – 2017

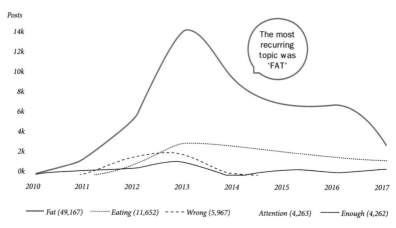

Data: Crimson Hexagon, 2017

Insecurity among young people - UK
Volume of posts (Emotion) from 2010 – 2017

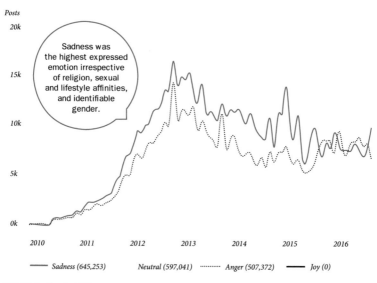

Data: Crimson Hexagon, 2017

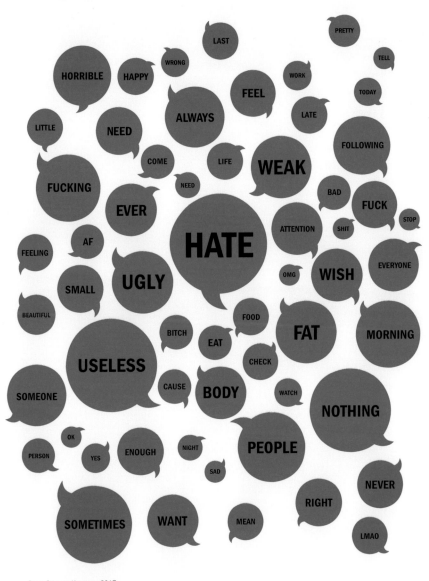

Data: Crimson Hexagon, 2017

RESOURCES

Creating your own PEEL project

Notes to workshop leaders

We often present ourselves on social media idealistically.
The process of online curation often fails to adequately reflect
our day-to-day reality or our true personalities.

PEEL seeks to reverse this trend by helping us to explore our
authentic selves through creative writing and photography.
It starts to address this issue by uncovering and expressing
deeper characteristics.

These next few pages are an introduction to the PEEL programme
that will help you set up your own PEEL project. By accessing all
the worksheets, you'll be able to run the project and manage the
results and output. The online resource will also provide you with
suggestions, tips and ideas of how to create the poems which will
inspire unique photographic portraits.

www.projectpeel.org

Programme

Set up

Running the project

Results & output

Poetry

Exploring ideas

The interview

Writing the poem

Photography

Exploring ideas

Using light

Framing & composition

The Programme

If you are a teacher or youth group leader, the full programme and worksheets can be downloaded at no cost.

To get started, go to the PEEL website and download your request form, fill it out and send it back to us. We'll send you a free entry code to the programme and you can start planning your project. When you've completed the programme, please give us your feedback. We would love to hear from you.

For more information go to:

www.projectpeel.org

Poetry

Interpreting truth

Writing poetry can seem quite daunting to those who are unfamiliar with it – but the simple interview is a great way to generate ideas. The beauty of poetry is the way it can be rich in meaning and feeling without using too many words. Whether rhyming or free verse, innovative word choices, rhythm and techniques such as metaphor can spark curiosity and pave the way for numerous interpretations. The PEEL worksheets will guide you through each part of the process so that you can help shape stories into an interesting and poetic narrative. Here is a brief summary of the steps you can take to do this…

Getting started

Get the participants into pairs (boy/girl where possible). This project works best when the pairs don't know each other well, so bear this in mind when pairing them up.
5 mins

The participants then interview their partner using the questions provided, giving answers in as much detail as possible. Note that the questions are simply a guide. The participants can ask additional questions of their own and they do not have to answer anything that makes them feel uncomfortable.
45 mins

The participants now review their partner's answers, selecting interesting, surprising or funny details for extended conversation. Further information should be documented.
30 mins

Then they look at their partner's information – was there a strong theme? Did anything particularly stand out? Try and identify a focus, theme, topic or narrative – this will help structure their poem. Further information on the focus can be supplied by the partners.
5-10 mins

Now the participants should start writing down some ideas for their poem, this could be a mind map, sentences, a word bank, lines or a paragraph. Their partner can help here too.
15 mins

Look at some of the example poems to give you some ideas and discuss different styles of poetry and techniques which you could include. If participants are struggling to begin, it may be helpful for them to not initially think about 'writing a poem'. Treating the initial composition stages as free-writing, without immediate concern for poetic technique or line break, often provokes more natural verse.
45 mins

Ask the participants to start pulling content from their notes to continue building the poem – shuffle, restructure, add and amend as necessary. Look at some of the 'How I Wrote My Poem' sheets written by other participants to help you.
30 mins

Once their poem is complete, ask them to share the poem with their partner for peer review and make amendments as necessary.
15 mins

How I wrote my poem

by George Adamson for Bryony Collishaw

First, I interviewed Bryony. I noticed she responded with some similar answers to different questions, mostly about music and art. When it came to writing the poem, I chose some of the more prominent repetitive answers, and picked things that sounded, to me, quite poetic and that would work well.

I started the poem off almost like a story. Looking through answers to the questions, I picked some correlating things and chose words that could give lines of the poem several meanings. The mood of my poem started quite sad, but ended more hopeful and wistful.

A lot of the responses left a dark, almost insecure vibe, and I put this into the poem, but used what inspires Bryony and what she uses to stay happy and calm to contrast against that.

See George's poem overleaf

The world's outlook
on the things you do
and the way you do them,

music and retiring
into yourself.

The peace seen through
a green, wide angled view.

A moving image
and childish colours.

Three hours spent in the dark
looking back on that summer.

Bryony Collishaw
Poetry – George Adamson

Poetry check list

Interview subject

Pick out most interesting answers –
what is clearly most important to them?

Rephrase, combine and
reinterpret answers

Try contrasting darker and more
light-hearted answers

Consider the direction of the poem,
try to develop a sense of change, turn
or epiphany

Remember poetry is not an exact
science - break the rules, be creative
and compose naturally

For more information go to:

www.projectpeel.org

Photography – Marksteen Adamson

Photography

Capturing authenticity

The best portrait photographers in the world are very capable of taking portraits that are natural and real without making structural changes to the face and body. In fact, there is never a need to change the look of someone's face or body. It makes us look 'super human' and it no longer represents the person that was photographed. After a while we start to hate these pictures of ourselves as they represent an aspiration that we will never achieve. Put simply, these pictures have no authenticity. They represent a 'social perfection' that we have now become tired and exhausted from seeing and trying to be.

It has been fashionable for many years now to take out all the natural blemishes in portraits and smooth out the very characteristics that make us unique. Over the last two decades, many fashion photographs have been subjected to so much post-production correction that the models appear unnatural, almost to the point of looking like cartoon characters or androids.

Removing or correcting permanent characteristics like symmetry, size and weight, only re-enforces the notion that we should all look a similar way and that having individuality and personality with unique features is socially unacceptable.

The PEEL project wants to reverse this trend through a journey of discovery and an understanding of true identity.

Photography – Marksteen Adamson

How I took Jack's photo

by Sophie Croft

I came up with a variety of ideas to photograph Jack. As my poem was about Jack's fear of water, I knew I would take his photo at the reservoir. We wanted to add in a comical element, therefore we came up with the inflatable swan as a prop to contrast Jack's fear.

By preparing the shoot at 7 p.m. the lighting was better than at midday, which would have bleached out the photos. When taking each photo, I focused on Jack and then adjusted the camera to the frame I wanted, making sure to include his shoulders and some of the reeds in the frame. I did not feel confident using a camera before the shoot but I learnt a lot about focusing, lighting and composition. By the end of the shoot, I felt confident that I had taken some successful photos.

See Sophie's poem and photo on page 71

Photography check list

Re-read poem
_____

Highlight key words and phrases
_____

Write a list of facial expressions,
postures, props and backgrounds that
best represent the idea behind the poem
_____

Discuss ideas with each other before
selecting the best one
_____

Try and think about how your subject
is lit and where your light source is
coming from
_____

Take care to make sure the subject's
eyes are in focus
_____

Take several photographs from different
angles, experimenting with light
_____

Think carefully about the composition,
clutter in the background and how you
intend to frame the subject
_____

For more information go to:

www.projectpeel.org

ACKNOWLEDGEMENTS

A big thank you

The PEEL project has been three years in the making and there are many friends who have been on the journey together. This project would not have happened without the love, care and support from so many supporters and volunteers.

PROJECT TEAM

Marian Cramers
Olivia Tan
Indy Roberts
Fabio Thomas
Natalie Thomas
Freya-Marie Saleh
Prudence Bond
Steven Tatlow

SUPPORTERS

Ashley Cullishaw
Mike Horne
Louise Adamson
Lindsey Power
Phil Sharpe
Marc Edmunds
Fenton Smith
The Right Revd
Rachel Treweek,
Bishop of Gloucester
Lucy Taylor
Linda Johnston
Helen Fisher
Adam Thilthorpe
David Evans
Carl Harris
David Hudson
Julian Thomas
The Hospital Club
Dale Campbell

VOLUNTEERS

James Miller
Charles Tucker
Mirren Derby
Jemima Metcalf
George Ovenden
George Kitching
George Adamson

DESIGN TEAM

Marksteen Adamson
Scott McGuffie
Simon Dryland
Emily Kane
Hannah Mapleston

DIRECTOR

Marksteen Adamson

SPECIAL THANKS

A special thank you to all the participants who have contributed to the four PEEL project workshops between 2015 and 2017.

The PEEL project is a strictly not for profit programme intended for educational use.

© PEEL, 2017

Design and project concept:
© ArthurSteenHorneAdamson, 2017

PRINTING AND BINDING

The PEEL book
The PEEL postcard holder
Boss Print Ltd.

PEEL lenticular posters and postcards
HIVE Associates Ltd.

PAPER

Gardapat Klassica, 115gsm
Fenner Paper Company Limited

CAMERA EQUIPMENT USED

Film cameras:
Nikon FE, FM3a,
Lens: Nikon Nikkor 50mm f1.2
Film: Ilford XP2 400 ASA

Digital cameras:
Nikon D3,
Nikon Df,
Nikon D700, D800, D810,
Lenses: Nikon Nikkor 35mm f1.4,
Nikon Nikkor 50mm f1.4,
Nikon Micro Nikkor 60mm f2.8

Leica M240 & M10,
Lenses: Leica 35mm f/2 Summicron-M ASPH,
Leica 50mm APO-Summicron-M ASPH f/2.0

FIRST EDITION

Published in 2017 by:

The Big Cold Turkey Foundation
60 St. George's Place
Cheltenham
GL50 3PN

Telephone: 01242 574 111
E-mail: us@thebigcoldturkey.com
www.thebigcoldturkey.com

A CIP record of this book is available from
the British Library.

ISBN: 978-0-9927606-1-8

SPONSORS & SUPPORTERS

"It's easier to build strong children than to repair broken adults."

F. Douglass